TRAVEL G

BERMUDA

Discover the Secrets of the Atlantic Jewel | Your

Ultimate Journey through Bermuda

Brian K. Kirby

Copyright © 2023 by Brian K. Kirby

Disclaimer:

The information provided in this book is intended for general informational purposes only. The author and publisher are not liable for any actions taken or decisions made based on the information contained in this book. Readers should consult with a professional for any specific advice or guidance related to their circumstances.

TABLE OF CONTENTS

CHAPTER 1: INTRODUCTION

Bermuda, a true gem nestled in the crystal-clear waters of the Atlantic Ocean, awaits your discovery. With its stunning pink sand beaches, vibrant marine life, and rich cultural heritage, Bermuda beckons travelers worldwide. In this travel guide, we embark on a journey to uncover the secrets and treasures of this enchanting island.

Bermuda is a cluster of 181 islands, islets, and rocks in the North Atlantic. Despite its small size, this British Overseas Territory captivates visitors with its natural beauty, fascinating history, and warm hospitality. Known for its iconic pastel-colored cottages, lush green landscapes, and inviting turquoise waters, Bermuda offers an irresistible allure that will leave a lasting impression.

As you flip through the pages of this travel guide, you'll embark on an adventure far beyond the postcard-perfect images often associated with Bermuda. We will delve deep into the island's soul, uncovering hidden corners and shedding light on lesser-known attractions that are often overlooked.

Bermuda's significance lies not only in its breathtaking landscapes but also in its historical and cultural importance. Initially discovered by Spanish explorer Juan de Bermúdez in the early 16th century, the island has since played a pivotal role in maritime history and has seen influences from Native American tribes, European settlers, and African heritage. This blending of cultures has shaped Bermuda into the vibrant and diverse destination it is today.

Our travel guide is designed to be your ultimate companion, providing you with the tools and knowledge to make the most of your journey through Bermuda. From Horseshoe Bay's sun-drenched beaches to St. George's charming streets, we will navigate the island together, uncovering its hidden treasures and immersing ourselves in its unique atmosphere.

Throughout the guide, you can expect detailed insights into the top attractions and landmarks that define Bermuda. We will take you on an exploration of the island's natural wonders, from the awe-inspiring Crystal Caves to the lush gardens of the Botanical Gardens. Immerse yourself in the vibrant local culture as we navigate the bustling markets, sample delectable seafood delicacies, and attend colorful festivals that showcase the island's heritage.

But our journey doesn't end there. Practical tips and advice on accommodations, transportation, and safety will ensure a smooth and hassle-free experience. Whether you're a first-time visitor or a seasoned traveler, this guide will equip you with the knowledge you need to create memories that will last a lifetime.

Prepare yourself for a thrilling adventure that will awaken your senses, ignite your curiosity, and instill in you a profound appreciation for the wonders of Bermuda. Join me as we uncover the secrets of this Atlantic Jewel and immerse ourselves in its breathtaking beauty and captivating history.

As you turn the page and dive into the following chapters, get ready to embrace the allure of Bermuda like never before. From hidden gems to popular landmarks, from tranquil beaches to vibrant local culture, our travel guide will be your trusted companion throughout your ultimate journey through Bermuda.

Get ready to experience the magic of Bermuda firsthand. The adventure begins now.

CHAPTER 2: GENERAL
INFORMATION

This chapter will delve into important details about Bermuda to equip you with essential knowledge before your journey to the Atlantic Jewel. Let's explore the practical information you need to know about this enchanting destination.

Location:

Bermuda, a captivating British Overseas Territory, is in the North Atlantic Ocean. It is situated approximately 1,070 kilometers (665 miles) east of Cape Hatteras, North Carolina, and enjoys a unique and strategic position.

Climate:

Bermuda boasts a delightful subtropical climate characterized by mild winters and warm summers. The island enjoys moderate temperatures throughout the year, with the summer months (June to September) experiencing averages of 26-30°C (79-86°F), while the winter months (December to March) see temperatures ranging from 17-20°C (63-68°F). However, it's worth noting that Bermuda is prone to occasional hurricanes, with the hurricane season typically running from June to November.

Time Zone:

Bermuda operates on Atlantic Standard Time (AST), four hours behind Coordinated Universal Time (UTC-4). The island maintains a consistent time throughout the year without observing daylight saving time.

Currency:

The official currency of Bermuda is the Bermudian dollar (BMD), often denoted as "$" or "BD$." It is on par with the United States dollar (USD), and both currencies are widely accepted on the island. Be sure to have cash on hand, as not all establishments accept credit cards, especially in more remote areas.

Entry Requirements:

Before traveling to Bermuda, it's essential to understand the entry requirements. Visitors from certain countries may require a visa to enter Bermuda, while others may be eligible for visa-exempt entry. It is recommended to check with the nearest Bermudian embassy or consulate or visit the official Bermuda government website for the most up-to-date information regarding visa requirements based on nationality.

Additionally, all travelers must have a valid machine-readable passport. The passport should have at least six months of validity beyond the intended departure date from Bermuda.

Health and Safety:

Bermuda maintains high health and safety standards, and no specific vaccinations are required for entry. It is recommended to obtain travel insurance that includes coverage for medical expenses when traveling to Bermuda, as healthcare expenses can be costly. It's also a good practice to familiarize yourself with emergency contact numbers and any specific safety guidelines the local authorities provide.

Customs and Regulations:

When entering Bermuda, being aware of customs and regulations is important. Certain items, including firearms, illegal drugs, and certain types of food, may be restricted or prohibited from being brought into the country. Familiarize yourself with the customs regulations to avoid any inconveniences during your travel.

Now equipped with this valuable information, you are ready to embark on your journey to Bermuda. Prepare to immerse yourself in this Atlantic Jewel's natural wonders, rich culture, and warm hospitality.

CHAPTER 3: GETTING THERE

Embarking to Bermuda is like stepping into a realm of wonder and enchantment. With its stunning landscapes, captivating history, and warm island vibes, Bermuda beckons adventurers from around the globe. But before you can lose yourself in the beauty of this Atlantic Jewel, you need to know how to get there. Prepare for an exciting exploration of transportation options that will whisk you away to this extraordinary destination.

Imagine soaring through the skies, your anticipation building as the airplane descends towards the captivating island of Bermuda. Your heart quickens with each passing moment, knowing you're about to step into a paradise unlike any other. L.F. Wade International Airport (BDA) welcomes you with open arms, offering a gateway to an unforgettable adventure.

The warm Bermuda breeze greets you as you leave the plane, carrying the promise of sandy beaches and turquoise waters. The possibilities are endless, and now it's time to choose your mode of transportation to reach your accommodation and explore the wonders that await.

Standing in vibrant hues, taxis line up outside the airport, ready to whisk you away to your destination. The friendly drivers, with their wealth of local knowledge, are eager to share stories and recommendations as they navigate the island's winding roads. Feel the excitement build as you catch glimpses of picturesque villages, swaying palm trees, and the azure ocean stretching out before you.

But if you're looking for a more adventurous approach, public buses await, ready to transport you to every corner of Bermuda. The island's well-connected bus network ensures that every beach, historical site, and charming town is within reach. As you board the bus, join the local chatter, and take in the scenery passing by. You'll immerse yourself in the vibrant tapestry of Bermuda's culture and daily life.

For those who yearn for the freedom to explore at their own pace, scooter and bicycle rentals offer a thrilling alternative.

Picture yourself zipping along winding coastal roads, the wind in your hair, as you discover hidden coves, secret lookout points, and secluded beaches. Feel the refreshing sense of independence as you navigate the island's picturesque trails, with each pedal or twist of the throttle bringing you closer to unforgettable experiences.

The sun setting over the horizon creates a beautiful golden glow over the island, and the ferries in Bermuda are calling to me. Step aboard and set sail across the glistening waters, taking in breathtaking views of Bermuda's coastline from a different perspective. With the wind in your face and the gentle rocking of the boat beneath you, you'll feel a sense of tranquility as you traverse between the island's iconic destinations.

And for those seeking the comfort of their wheels, car rentals provide the ultimate flexibility. Imagine driving along Bermuda's scenic routes, stopping whenever a breathtaking vista captures your attention. Renting a car allows you to explore beyond the popular routes, discovering hidden treasures and making unforgettable experiences on this enchanting island.

But the transportation options continue. Private boats and yachts find solace in Bermuda's inviting waters, allowing you to arrive in style and explore the island's hidden coves and secluded anchorages. And for the curious souls who prefer guided experiences, tours, and excursions cater to every interest, offering a curated journey through Bermuda's treasures with transportation seamlessly arranged.

So, whether you choose to arrive by air, traverse the island by bus, scooter, or rental car, or explore the coastlines by boat, Bermuda's transportation options ensure that your adventure starts from the moment you arrive. Get ready to immerse yourself in this Atlantic Jewel's beauty, history, and vibrant spirit as you embark on your ultimate journey through Bermuda. Let the transportation choices ignite your exploration and pave the way for unforgettable moments that await around every corner.

CHAPTER 4: ACCOMMODATION

Imagine stepping into your oasis, a haven that embraces you with comfort and luxury as you embark on your unforgettable journey through Bermuda. In this chapter of "Travel Guide Bermuda: Discover the Secrets of the Atlantic Jewel," we will delve into the world of accommodations that await you on this enchanting island. Get ready to indulge in the perfect retreat that complements your desires, preferences, and budget, ensuring an extraordinary experience from the moment you step through the doors.

As you arrive in Bermuda, the anticipation builds, and the allure of the island's pristine beaches, vibrant culture, and captivating history beckons you. Your choice of accommodation plays a pivotal role in shaping your overall experience, providing a sanctuary to recharge and immerse yourself in the island's magic.

Bermuda caters to all types of travelers, whether you seek opulent luxury or a more budget-friendly option that allows you to allocate your resources toward exciting adventures and exploration. From grand resorts to charming guesthouses, boutique hotels, and unique vacation rentals, the island presents many choices, each promising a memorable stay.

Picture yourself stepping into a luxurious hotel where impeccable service, lavish amenities, and stunning ocean views redefine the meaning of indulgence. Bermuda boasts an impressive selection of world-class hotels and resorts, offering opulent suites, exquisite dining options, and private beach access. From iconic establishments to hidden gems, these accommodations epitomize elegance and sophistication, ensuring an unparalleled level of comfort and pampering throughout your stay.

If you prefer a more intimate and authentic experience, consider staying at one of Bermuda's charming guesthouses. Nestled in picturesque neighborhoods and immersed in local culture, these accommodations offer a warm and welcoming atmosphere. Embrace the personal touch and genuine hospitality as you connect with fellow travelers and the friendly hosts who share their insider tips and local knowledge, providing a genuinely authentic Bermuda experience.

For budget-conscious travelers, hostels provide a comfortable and affordable option, allowing you to stretch your resources further while fostering a sense of community and camaraderie. Ideal for solo adventurers or those seeking a social environment, hostels offer shared dormitories or private rooms and communal spaces where you can connect with fellow travelers, exchange stories, and forge lasting friendships.

For a unique and immersive experience, consider booking a vacation rental, which allows you to live like a local during your stay in Bermuda. Whether it's a cozy cottage, a stylish apartment, or a charming villa, vacation rentals offer a home-away-from-home ambiance, complete with fully equipped kitchens and living spaces. They provide the flexibility and freedom to create your schedule while savoring the island's beauty at your own pace.

When booking accommodations in Bermuda, there are a few tips to keep in mind. First, consider the location that best aligns with your preferences. Whether you desire the vibrant energy of Hamilton, the tranquility of the East End, or the allure of the South Shore's breathtaking beaches, choose an area that complements your itinerary and desired atmosphere.

Additionally, consider the amenities that are important to you, such as beach access, pools, on-site restaurants, or spa facilities. Some accommodations offer complimentary water sports equipment or access to golf courses, ensuring your desires for adventure and leisure are met.

As you embark on your search for the perfect accommodation, take advantage of online travel platforms, hotel websites, and reputable booking agents to compare prices, read reviews, and secure the best deals. Book well, especially during peak travel seasons, to ensure availability and reserve your preferred choice.

Whichever type of accommodation you choose, rest assured that Bermuda's commitment to hospitality and exceptional service will leave a lasting impression. From the moment you step foot into your chosen retreat, you'll feel the island's warmth and embrace, setting the stage for an unforgettable experience.

So, immerse yourself in Bermuda's accommodations, where luxury, charm, and comfort converge.

CHAPTER 5: ATTRACTIONS AND ACTIVITIES

As you step foot on the pristine shores of Bermuda, you'll find yourself immersed in a world of unparalleled beauty and rich history. The island is brimming with captivating attractions that will transport you through time, allowing you to unravel the secrets within its vibrant past. Brace yourself for an adventure that will take you from ancient fortresses to awe-inspiring caves, quaint cobblestone streets, and breathtaking pink sand beaches.

Let's begin our exploration by delving into the historical landmarks that make Bermuda unique. St. George's, a UNESCO World Heritage Site, will enchant you with its well-preserved colonial architecture, narrow lanes, and centuries-old churches. Walk in the footsteps of history as you visit the State House, the oldest continuously occupied legislative building in the New World, or explore the mighty ramparts of the UNESCO-listed Fort St. Catherine, guarding the island since the early 17th century.

Venture to the Royal Naval Dockyard, once a vital outpost of the British Empire, and uncover its fascinating past at the National Museum of Bermuda. Discover the iconic

Commissioner's House, once the residence of the highest-ranking naval officer, now transformed into a captivating museum that offers a glimpse into Bermuda's maritime heritage.

Nature lovers will be enthralled by the island's natural wonders, starting with the awe-inspiring Crystal Caves. Descend into a subterranean world of dazzling stalactites and turquoise pools, marveling at these limestone formations' sheer beauty and geological significance. And don't miss the neighboring Fantasy Caves, where the ethereal beauty of stalagmites and underground lakes will leave you breathless.

No trip to Bermuda is complete without visiting its renowned pink sand beaches. Come and experience the powdery soft sands and mesmerizing turquoise waters of Horseshoe Bay Beach. Enjoy some relaxation under the sun, and take a refreshing dip in the Atlantic. Elbow Beach, with its tranquil ambiance and natural beauty, offers a serene escape where you can unwind and reconnect with nature.

But Bermuda offers more than just stunning landscapes and historical landmarks. It's a playground for adventure enthusiasts and thrill-seekers alike. Dive into the vibrant underwater world as you snorkel or scuba dive among colorful coral reefs teeming with marine life. Explore ancient shipwrecks, remnants of Bermuda's treacherous coastline and witness history frozen in time beneath the waves.

For those seeking adrenaline-pumping activities, Bermuda's waters offer jet skiing, parasailing, paddleboarding, and kiteboarding opportunities. Feel the rush as you skim across the crystal-clear waves, immersing yourself in the exhilarating energy of the Atlantic.

Enjoy Bermuda's vibrant culture by joining a guided tour of its traditions and local customs. Explore the bustling markets, sample delectable seafood delicacies, and learn about the island's artistic heritage. Be captivated by the pulsating rhythms of Gombey dancers, a colorful display of Bermuda's African roots and cultural pride.

To connect with the island's essence:

1. Consider partaking in a local experience.
2. Interact with the amiable locals, who are constantly willing to share their tales and show you their preferred hidden treasures.
3. Join a fishing excursion and try catching your dinner, or indulge in a sunset cruise, where you can

revel in the serenity and beauty of Bermuda's coastal vistas.

Whether you immerse yourself in history, embrace the thrill of adventure, or delve into the vibrant culture, Bermuda offers many attractions and activities that cater to every traveler's desires. Let your curiosity guide you as you create your extraordinary journey through this Atlantic Jewel.

As you plan your itinerary, consider joining guided tours or seeking the expertise of local guides who can provide valuable insights and enrich your experience with their extensive knowledge. Please take advantage of their expertise to uncover hidden gems and experience the island through the eyes of a true Bermudian.

CHAPTER 6: DINING AND ENTERTAINMENT

In this chapter, we dive into the vibrant world of dining and entertainment that awaits you on this captivating island. Get ready to indulge in a tantalizing array of flavors, experience the rich cultural tapestry through food, and immerse yourself in the vibrant entertainment scene that will leave you craving more.

Bermuda is a visual feast for the eyes and a paradise for food enthusiasts. From delectable seafood delicacies to mouthwatering international cuisines, the island boasts a diverse culinary landscape that reflects its rich history and cultural heritage. Prepare to embark on a gastronomic journey that will delight your senses and leave you with unforgettable culinary memories.

Let's start our culinary exploration by delving into the local cuisine of Bermuda. The island's culinary scene is deeply rooted in its maritime heritage, emphasizing fresh seafood. Indulge in succulent rockfish, pan-seared scallops, or traditional Bermudian fish chowder, bursting with flavors and aromas that will transport you straight to the Atlantic coast.

As you traverse the island, sample other local delights such as codfish and potatoes, a beloved breakfast dish, or the savory Bermuda fish sandwich layered with fresh catch, tartar sauce, and crispy lettuce. Don't forget to try the iconic rum cake, infused with the island's famous Gosling's Black Seal Rum, offering a sweet and decadent taste of Bermuda.

Bermuda also embraces international influences, with many international cuisines to satisfy every palate. Indulge in Italian trattorias, where you can savor handmade pasta and wood-fired pizzas, or explore Asian fusion restaurants offering a blend of flavors from the Far East with a Bermudian twist. From French bistros to Mediterranean eateries, the culinary offerings in Bermuda are as diverse as they are delicious.

For a taste of local culture, venture into Bermuda's vibrant street food scene. Explore the bustling markets and street stalls, where you can sample traditional favorites such as fish cakes, Bermuda's answer to the fish fritter, or savory codfish balls, served piping hot and bursting with flavor. Take advantage of the Bermuda fish sandwich stands, where you can savor this island classic in a casual, on-the-go setting.

Beyond the tantalizing flavors of Bermuda, the island offers a vibrant entertainment scene that caters to all tastes. As the sun sets over the Atlantic, the island comes alive with many options for nightlife, cultural events, and entertainment.

For those seeking a vibrant nightlife experience, Hamilton, the island's capital, is a hub of activity. Discover lively bars and chic lounges, where you can sip on crafted cocktails and mingle with locals and fellow travelers alike. Dance the night away to live music or DJ sets that span various genres, from reggae and calypso to jazz and contemporary hits.

Enjoy the island's rich cultural heritage by attending local events and festivals. From the Bermuda Festival of the Performing Arts, showcasing world-class theater, dance, and music, to the Gombey troupes that take to the streets, blending African and British traditions into a mesmerizing spectacle, the cultural events in Bermuda offer a glimpse into the island's vibrant soul.

For theater enthusiasts, the Bermuda Musical and Dramatic Society stages captivating productions throughout the year, featuring talented local actors and visiting performers. Experience the magic of live theater in historic venues that transport you back and create memories that will stay long after the final curtain falls.

Music lovers will be enthralled by the island's vibrant music scene, which encompasses a range of genres, from traditional island rhythms to contemporary sounds. Explore music venues and beach bars where local bands and international artists perform, filling the air with melodic notes and infectious energy.

As you plan your visit to Bermuda, watch for special events and festivals during your travel period. From food festivals celebrating the island's culinary delights to cultural exhibitions that showcase local art and traditions, these events provide unique opportunities to immerse yourself in the vibrant fabric of Bermuda.

To enhance your dining and entertainment experiences, consider joining local food tours or cultural excursions that offer insider access to the best culinary hotspots and cultural landmarks. Engage with passionate locals eager to share their stories, traditions, and culinary expertise, allowing you to appreciate the island's rich cultural tapestry better.

From the tantalizing flavors that will ignite your taste buds to the pulsating rhythm of Bermuda's entertainment scene, the island offers a sensory feast that will leave you wanting more. So, indulge in the culinary delights, savor every bite, and immerse yourself in the vibrant entertainment options that will make your journey through Bermuda unforgettable.

CHAPTER 7: SHOPPING AND
SOUVENIRS

Bermuda boasts a variety of shopping districts, each with its unique charm and offerings. Let's begin our shopping exploration by venturing into Hamilton's capital city. Front Street, the heart of Hamilton, is a bustling hub with many shops, boutiques, and department stores. You'll find everything from high-end fashion brands and jewelry to specialty stores showcasing local artisans and their handicrafts here. Stroll along the picturesque waterfront, taking in the city's vibrant energy as you browse the shops for that perfect memento.

Another popular shopping destination is the Royal Naval Dockyard, which combines history, entertainment, and retail therapy. This vibrant area is home to numerous shops, where you can find everything from locally-made products to international brands. Explore the Clocktower Mall within the Dockyard, which houses various shops, including art galleries, souvenir stores, and unique boutiques offering handmade crafts and jewelry. Take a leisurely walk through the mall, soaking in the historical atmosphere as you peruse the diverse offerings.

For a different shopping experience, venture to the charming town of St. George's. This site, recognized by UNESCO as a World Heritage Site, combines history with shopping in a distinct and special way. Wander through the quaint streets lined with colorful buildings, and discover local shops offering a range of goods, including artwork, handmade crafts, and locally-produced items. Take advantage of the historic Somers Wharf, where you can find a collection of shops and boutiques offering a variety of souvenirs and gifts.

If you want a more traditional shopping experience, head to one of Bermuda's modern shopping malls. The Mall at Marathon, located in the island's heart, features a range of stores offering clothing, accessories, and electronics. Here, you can find well-known international brands and enjoy a relaxed shopping environment.

While exploring Bermuda's shopping districts, watch for unique local products and handicrafts that make for wonderful souvenirs. Bermuda is famous for its beautiful handcrafted items, including cedar woodwork, pottery, and hand-woven baskets. These locally-made crafts reflect the island's rich cultural heritage and make for meaningful and authentic keepsakes.

Cedar woodwork, intricately carved and polished, is a Bermudian specialty. From jewelry boxes and picture frames to ornaments and sculptures, these exquisite pieces showcase the craftsmanship and artistry of local artisans. Look for reputable shops offering high-quality cedar woodwork, ensuring you bring home a genuine part of Bermuda's heritage.

Pottery is another popular local craft, with unique designs and vibrant colors that reflect the island's natural beauty.

From decorative vases to functional tableware, Bermudian pottery adds a touch of island flair to any home. Visit local pottery studios or artisan markets to discover these beautiful creations and support the local artistic community.

Hand-woven baskets, known as "Bermuda bags," are iconic island symbols. Crafted from natural materials such as palmetto and sisal, these baskets showcase the traditional weaving techniques passed down through generations. They make for both practical and decorative souvenirs, serving as a reminder of Bermuda's rich cultural heritage.

When shopping in Bermuda, keeping a few tips in mind is helpful. While bargaining is not common in most retail establishments, some local artisans or vendors at markets may be open to negotiation. It's always polite to inquire about prices and respectfully discuss the possibility of a discount if appropriate. Remember that establishing a friendly rapport can go a long way in securing the best deal.

As you explore the shopping scene in Bermuda, take your time to browse, compare prices, and interact with the local shopkeepers. They can provide valuable insights into the products and help you find that perfect item to take home. Don't hesitate to ask questions or seek recommendations—they are passionate about their craft and eager to share their knowledge with visitors.

Before purchasing, remember customs regulations or restrictions on bringing certain items back to your home country. Some products, such as coral, shells, or endangered animal products, may be subject to restrictions or require permits. Familiarize yourself with the relevant guidelines to ensure a smooth return journey.

Shopping in Bermuda is not just about acquiring material possessions; it's about immersing yourself in the island's culture, supporting local artisans, and creating lasting memories. So, wander through the vibrant shopping districts, explore the boutiques and markets, and bring home a piece of Bermuda's charm that will forever remind you of your ultimate journey through the Atlantic Jewel.

CHAPTER 8: SAFETY AND HEALTH

Let's begin by exploring some general safety tips for your Bermuda experience. While Bermuda is generally considered a safe destination, it's important to exercise caution and remain vigilant, just as you would in any new environment. Keep your personal belongings secure at all times, ensuring valuables are safely stored and out of sight. By being mindful of your surroundings and avoiding displaying valuable items, you can minimize the risk of theft or pickpocketing.

Scams and petty theft can be found in any popular tourist destination, and Bermuda is no exception. Stay alert and cautious when approached by strangers offering unsolicited services or deals that seem too good to be true. Always verify prices before purchasing, and opt for reputable vendors and establishments. By using your judgment and relying on trusted sources, you can avoid scams and enjoy a worry-free shopping and dining experience.

Respecting local customs and traditions is a sign of courtesy and an essential aspect of staying safe and maintaining positive interactions with the local community. Familiarize yourself with the cultural norms of Bermuda, dress appropriately when visiting religious sites or conservative areas, and be mindful of local sensitivities. Greet locals with a warm smile and observe social norms to foster a harmonious and respectful connection with the Bermudian people.

Regarding transportation, prioritize your safety by following guidelines and regulations. Whether using public transportation, taxis, or rental vehicles, it's crucial to buckle up and adhere to traffic laws. If you explore the island on a rented scooter or bicycle, ensure you have the necessary skills and licenses. Familiarize yourself with local road conditions and exercise caution, always prioritizing your well-being and that of fellow road users.

Rest assured that Bermuda is well-equipped with emergency services to ensure your safety throughout your journey. In case of emergencies or to report a crime, dial 911 to reach the Bermuda Police Service. They are dedicated to maintaining law and order on the island and are readily available to assist with any safety concerns or incidents.

Bermuda offers a range of healthcare services for medical emergencies to ensure your well-being. The main hospital, King Edward VII Memorial Hospital, provides emergency care, general medical services, and specialized treatments. Additionally, private medical clinics and urgent care centers are scattered across the island. Having comprehensive travel insurance that covers medical expenses, emergency medical evacuation, and trip cancellation or interruption is of utmost importance. Familiarize yourself with your policy's coverage and keep copies of your insurance documents easily accessible during your trip.

Before traveling to Bermuda, you should ensure you are up-to-date on routine vaccinations. Consult with a healthcare professional or travel medicine specialist to determine if additional vaccinations are recommended based on your health condition and travel plans. While the likelihood of contracting mosquito-borne diseases in Bermuda is minimal, it is still wise to take precautionary steps. These include using insect repellent and wearing appropriate clothing to prevent mosquito bites.

When in Bermuda, it is important to take sun safety precautions due to the abundant sunshine. To avoid harmful UV rays, consider wearing sunscreen with a high SPF, seeking shade during peak sun hours, and wearing a wide-brimmed hat and sunglasses. Stay hydrated to prevent dehydration and heat-related illnesses, particularly in warmer months.

By staying informed, following safety tips, and taking necessary health precautions, you can ensure a smooth and secure journey through Bermuda. Embrace the wonders of this Atlantic Jewel with the confidence that your well-being is prioritized and you are equipped with the knowledge to navigate any situation. So, get ready to explore, indulge, and create lifelong memories in Bermuda, knowing that your safety and health are in good hands as you embark on your ultimate journey through this captivating destination.

CHAPTER 9: LOCAL TRANSPORTATION

Imagine hopping onto a colorful bus, the vibrant hues reflecting the island's spirit, as it takes you on a winding journey through Bermuda's captivating landscapes. The bus system in Bermuda is not just a mode of transport but a gateway to adventure. Step aboard and let the rhythmic motion of the bus carry you from one stunning destination to another. Marvel at the scenic beauty outside your window, from the iconic pink sand beaches to the lush greenery that blankets the island. With its extensive network of routes, the bus system opens up a world of possibilities, allowing you to explore hidden gems and vibrant communities at your own pace.

But the excitement doesn't end with buses alone. Bermuda's ferry service offers a unique and enchanting way to traverse the crystal-clear waters that surround the island. Picture yourself on the open deck of a ferry, the sea breeze gently caressing your face as you sail past picturesque harbors and secluded coves. The ferry system connects various points within Bermuda, providing a practical means of transportation and a front-row seat to the breathtaking coastal scenery. Let the ferry become your passport to adventure as you hop from one enchanting destination to the next, discovering the wonders of Bermuda.

For those seeking a more independent and adventurous experience, Bermuda opens its doors to bicycles and scooters. Feel the wind in your hair as you pedal along picturesque trails and explore the island's hidden corners on two wheels. Bermuda's network of bike-friendly roads and pathways beckons you to embark on a journey of discovery, where every turn reveals a new vista of natural beauty and cultural treasures. Alternatively, rent a scooter and embrace the freedom of the open road. Feel the thrill of exploration as you zip along Bermuda's coastal roads, uncovering secret beaches, charming towns, and breathtaking viewpoints. With every twist and turn, you'll feel a sense of liberation and a connection to the island that is truly unparalleled.

Of course, if you prefer a more relaxed and convenient mode of transportation, taxis are readily available throughout Bermuda. Hail a taxi, and allow yourself to be whisked away to your desired destination easily and comfortably. The friendly and knowledgeable taxi drivers will get you where you need to go and share fascinating stories and local insights along the way. Take a seat, unwind, and soak in the beauty and sounds of Bermuda while riding comfortably in a taxi, as you explore the island's colorful fabric.

As you plan your transportation adventures, keep in mind some helpful tips. Familiarize yourself with bus and ferry schedules, optimizing your time and minimizing waiting. Consider purchasing transportation tokens or passes for convenience and cost savings if you plan to use buses or ferries frequently. Embrace the Bermudian way of life and allow for a touch of flexibility in your schedule. Take a deep breath, soak in the island's charm, and savor the moments of unexpected discovery that can happen when you let go of rigid itineraries.

Bermuda's transportation system is not just about getting from point A to point B—it's about embracing the journey and immersing yourself in the essence of the island. It's about anticipating what lies around the next bend, the thrill of exploring new places, and the freedom to create your adventure. So, whether you choose to ride the buses, sail on the ferries, pedal on bicycles, zip on scooters, or cruise in taxis, let the excitement of local transportation be an integral part of your ultimate journey through the Atlantic Jewel that is Bermuda.

CHAPTER 10: LANGUAGE AND COMMUNICATION

Imagine stepping onto the sun-kissed shores of Bermuda, the air buzzing with excitement and anticipation. As you venture into this Atlantic Jewel's heart, the spoken language is a gateway to cultural immersion and meaningful connections. English, the official language of Bermuda, is your passport to seamless communication with the local community. Feel the warmth of Bermudian hospitality as you engage in conversations, exchange smiles, and unlock the treasure trove of experiences that await you.

While English may be the predominant language in Bermuda, it's always fun and enriching to learn a few basic phrases to enhance your interactions and demonstrate your interest in the local culture. So, let's embark on a linguistic adventure and uncover some useful phrases that will undoubtedly bring a smile to the faces of Bermudians you encounter along your journey.

"Hello" - A simple greeting that opens the door to friendly exchanges. A warm "Hello" or "Good day" in Bermuda will instantly break the ice and make you feel at home.

"Thank you" - Expressing gratitude is a universal language. Saying "Thank you" or "Thank you very much" in Bermuda ("T'ank you" or "T'ank you berry much") will undoubtedly be appreciated and leave a lasting impression.

"Excuse me" is a polite phrase to use when seeking assistance or getting someone's attention. Whether you're asking for directions or navigating through a crowd, a polite "Excuse me" ("Pardon me") will ensure a smooth flow of communication.

"Please" - A magical word that adds a touch of politeness and respect to any request. Remember to say "Please" ("Pleez") when seeking assistance or making a polite inquiry.

"Do you speak English?" - Although English is widely spoken in Bermuda, asking "Do you speak English?" ("Do ya speak English?") shows your willingness to adapt and respect the local language customs.

These simple phrases will undoubtedly enhance your interactions and create a positive connection with the people of Bermuda. As you engage in conversations, embrace the island's vibrant spirit and allow the language to bridge cultures and foster meaningful connections.

In addition to language, communication in the modern age often involves staying connected through mobile networks and internet access. Regarding mobile network coverage in Bermuda, the island offers reliable and widespread connectivity. Major mobile network providers have ranged across the island, ensuring you can stay connected and share your incredible Bermuda experiences with friends and family back home.

To stay connected during your journey, consider obtaining a local SIM card. SIM cards are readily available at various locations, including airports, tourist information centers, and mobile network provider stores. Purchasing a local SIM card can offer you the convenience of affordable local calls, data services, and access to the internet while exploring the Atlantic Jewel.

Internet access is also widely available in Bermuda. Many accommodations, restaurants, cafes, and public areas offer free Wi-Fi, allowing you to stay connected and share your Bermuda adventures easily. Check with your accommodation provider or inquire about Wi-Fi availability and any login requirements at local establishments.

While staying connected is valuable, we encourage you to find a balance between experiencing the beauty of Bermuda firsthand and enjoying the digital world. Take moments to disconnect, immerse yourself in the stunning surroundings, and fully embrace the island's charm.

So, as you embark on your linguistic and digital voyage through Bermuda, let language be your guide to cultural immersion and connection. Engage in conversations, share laughter, and unlock the secrets of this enchanting island.

Stay connected, but take moments to unplug and fully experience the magic surrounding you. Let language and communication be the threads that weave your Bermuda memories into a tapestry of unforgettable experiences.

CHAPTER 11: TRAVEL TIPS AND ETIQUETTE

Picture yourself standing at the edge of a pink sand beach, the sun casting a golden glow on the crystal-clear waters that stretch as far as the eye can see. As you take in the breathtaking beauty of Bermuda, you realize that a smooth and well-prepared travel experience is the key to unlocking the full potential of this Atlantic Jewel. By acquiring the necessary knowledge and guidance, navigating the island, building genuine relationships with the natives, and completely submerging yourself in the lively culture around you can be effortlessly accomplished.

Before you embark on your journey, let's start with packing suggestions to set the stage for a comfortable and enjoyable stay. Bermuda's mild climate calls for lightweight clothing that allows you to embrace the island's warmth and enjoy the cool ocean breeze. Fill your suitcase with cotton shirts, shorts, dresses, and swimwear as you prepare to explore the stunning beaches and picturesque landscapes. Remember to pack sunscreen, hats, and sunglasses to protect yourself from the sun's rays. And remember, a light jacket or sweater will come in handy for cooler evenings, ensuring your comfort as you savor Bermuda's captivating charm.

As you plan your adventure, it's important to consider the weather and its seasonal variations. Bermuda's year-round mild climate offers different experiences throughout the seasons. Whether you're basking in the warmth of summer, enjoying the mild temperatures of spring and fall, or embracing the gentle winter months, knowing what to expect will help you make the most of your time on the island. Layering your clothing and having a mix of light and warmer attire will allow you to adapt to changing weather conditions and fully enjoy all that Bermuda offers.

But travel is not just about what you pack—it's about how you engage with the local culture and community. Bermuda has a rich heritage and a set of customs that add depth and meaning to your journey. Following a few simple guidelines, you can navigate the island respectfully and create meaningful connections with the Bermudian people.

Greetings are the gateway to cultural immersion. A warm "Hello" or "Good day" sets the tone for positive interactions and shows your interest in connecting with the local community. Embrace the Bermudian way of politeness and hospitality, and be sure to say "please" and "thank you" as you navigate the island. These simple gestures go a long way in building rapport and creating memorable experiences.

Tipping is customary in Bermuda and a way to show appreciation for good service. It's customary to leave a gratuity of 15-20% of the total bill when dining in restaurants unless a service charge has already been included. Tipping based on the level of service received is customary and appreciated for other services, such as taxis or hotel staff.

As you explore Bermuda's stunning beaches and vibrant communities, it's important to be mindful of appropriate behavior. Respect the environment by disposing trash in designated bins and following specific beach rules or restrictions. Dress modestly and respectfully in public places, especially when visiting religious sites or attending formal events. By adhering to these guidelines, you demonstrate your appreciation for the local customs and contribute to a harmonious and positive travel experience for everyone.

As you immerse yourself in the wonders of Bermuda, remember to engage with the locals, ask questions, and listen to their stories. Embrace the spirit of curiosity and openness, and let the culture of Bermuda envelop you in its vibrant embrace. By honoring the customs and etiquette of the island, you'll forge connections that transcend language and create lasting memories of your time in this captivating destination.

So, as you prepare to embark on your ultimate journey through Bermuda, armed with practical tips, weather considerations, and cultural etiquette, get ready to unlock the secrets of a truly extraordinary experience. Pack your suitcase with anticipation, respect the island's traditions, and open your heart to Bermuda's warmth and beauty. It's time to set sail on a voyage of discovery, where every encounter, every greeting, and every respectful gesture opens doors to the hidden treasures of the Atlantic Jewel.

CHAPTER 12: MAPS AND ITINERARIES

In this chapter, we embark on a visual journey through maps and create a roadmap for your ultimate adventure in Bermuda. Whether you're a first-time visitor or returning to uncover more of the island's hidden gems, we have you covered. Get ready to explore a comprehensive Bermuda map highlighting key attractions, transportation hubs, and recommended routes. Additionally, we'll provide sample itineraries tailored to suit different durations and the diverse interests of travelers like you.

Map of Bermuda

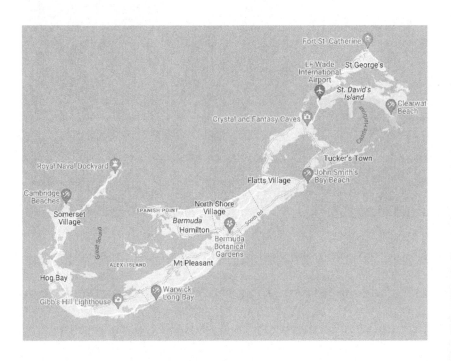

Sample Itineraries

We've created sample itineraries tailored to different durations and interests to make the most of your time in Bermuda. Whether you're seeking adventure, relaxation, cultural immersion, or a combination of all three, these itineraries provide a blueprint for your unforgettable journey.

a) 3-Day Itinerary: This itinerary is perfect for a short getaway, allowing you to experience the essence of Bermuda in a condensed timeframe. Day 1 can be dedicated to exploring the historical treasures of St. George's, a UNESCO World Heritage Site. Day 2 can be spent discovering the vibrant capital city of Hamilton, with its charming streets, boutiques, and cultural attractions. Finally, Day 3 can be devoted to beach hopping as you soak in the beauty of Bermuda's renowned pink sand beaches and indulge in water sports or relaxation.

b) 7-Day Itinerary: With a week to spare, you can delve deeper into Bermuda's diverse offerings. In addition to exploring St. George's and Hamilton, this itinerary allows you to venture to the Royal Naval Dockyard, a hub of entertainment, shopping, and historical significance. You'll also have time to explore Bermuda's nature reserves, hike scenic trails, and savor the local cuisine. Furthermore, this itinerary offers opportunities for day trips to nearby islands, such as the picturesque Somerset Island or the secluded paradise of Nonsuch Island.

c) 14-Day Itinerary: A two-week itinerary is ideal for the ultimate immersion in Bermuda's treasures. This extended journey allows you to explore the lesser-known gems of the island, including charming villages, hidden coves, and local cultural experiences. You can venture beyond the main island and discover the enchanting islands of the Bermuda archipelago, each offering unique charm and attractions. With two weeks at your disposal, you'll have the time to fully embrace Bermuda's relaxed pace of life, engage with the local community, and uncover the secrets that lie off the beaten path.

These sample itineraries serve as a starting point for your own customized adventure. Feel free to mix and match attractions, add your interests, and allow serendipity to guide you as you explore Bermuda's wonders.

As you embark on your journey armed with our detailed map and expertly crafted itineraries, remember that flexibility and spontaneity are key to discovering the hidden gems of Bermuda. Take detours, follow your instincts, and be open to unexpected encounters. Let the map be your guide, but allow the spirit of exploration to lead you to unexpected discoveries that will make your journey extraordinary.

CHAPTER 13: USEFUL CONTACTS

This chapter provides you with a comprehensive list of important contacts that will ensure a safe, informed, and enjoyable journey through Bermuda. From local tourism offices to embassy contacts and emergency hotlines, having access to these essential numbers will give you peace of mind as you explore the wonders of this captivating destination.

1. Local Tourism Offices:

Local tourism offices are your go-to resources when seeking information, guidance, or assistance in Bermuda. These offices are staffed with knowledgeable professionals passionate about sharing Bermuda's best with visitors. They can provide up-to-date information on attractions, events, transportation, and other inquiries.

Here are the contact details for the local tourism offices in Bermuda:

- Bermuda Tourism Authority:

 - Website: www.gotobermuda.com

 - Phone: +1-800-882-4BDA (4232)

- Bermuda Department of Tourism:

- Website: www.bermudatourism.com

- Phone: +1-441-292-0023

2. Embassies or Consulates:

While Bermuda is a British Overseas Territory, it has its distinct government and administration. Bermuda's defense and foreign affairs are under the responsibility of the United Kingdom. If you require consular assistance or have any diplomatic inquiries, it's advisable to contact the nearest British embassy or consulate.

Here are the contact details for the British embassy and consulate in Bermuda:

- British Embassy in Bermuda:

- Phone: +1-441-299-6566

- Address: Crown Hill, 42 North Shore Road, Hamilton Parish HS1 1 5, Bermuda

3. Emergency Hotlines:

In case of emergencies or immediate assistance, it's crucial to have access to the relevant emergency hotlines. Whether you require medical attention, police assistance, or any other emergency services, the following numbers will connect you to the appropriate authorities:

- Police (Emergency): 911

- Ambulance (Emergency): 911

- Fire (Emergency): 911

4. Non-Emergency Contacts:

For non-emergency situations, it's helpful to have additional contact information readily available. Here are some non-emergency numbers that may be useful during your stay in Bermuda:

- Non-Emergency Police: +1-441-295-0011

- Bermuda Hospitals Board (General Enquiries): +1-441-236-2345

5. Consular Contacts:

Suppose you're a citizen of a country other than the United Kingdom and require consular assistance. In that case, having the contact information for your country's embassy or consulate in Bermuda is recommended. These consular offices can provide support and guidance in case of lost passports, legal issues, or other consular matters. Ensure you have the relevant contact details before your journey.

6. Local Emergency Services and Hospital:

In a medical emergency, it's essential to have the contact information for local emergency services and hospitals. These numbers can be invaluable if you or someone in your party requires immediate medical attention.

Here are the contacts for emergency medical services and hospitals in Bermuda:

- Bermuda Hospitals Board (King Edward VII Memorial Hospital - Emergency): +1-441-236-2345

Remember, it's always a good idea to save these contact numbers in your phone or keep them easily accessible during your stay in Bermuda. Having these numbers at your fingertips in an emergency or when you need assistance will ensure prompt and appropriate support.

As you venture into the wonders of Bermuda, keep this list of useful contacts as a valuable resource. The local tourism offices will provide guidance and information to enhance your experience, while the embassy and consular contacts will offer support if needed. The emergency hotlines and non-emergency contacts will give you peace of mind, knowing that help is just a phone call away.

So, as you embark on your ultimate journey through Bermuda, armed with the knowledge of these essential contacts, rest assured that you have the resources to make your trip safe, informed, and enjoyable. Explore with confidence, knowing that you have the support of the local tourism offices, the consular services, and the emergency hotlines should you need them. Embrace the wonders of the Atlantic Jewel, knowing you can navigate any situation and make the most of your time in this captivating destination.

CHAPTER 14: ADDITIONAL

RESOURCES

In this chapter, we provide a curated list of additional resources to enhance your journey through Bermuda. From websites and guidebooks to helpful mobile apps, these resources provide valuable information, insider tips, and convenient tools to make the most of your time in this captivating destination.

1. Websites:

a) **Bermuda** **Tourism** **Authority** **(www.gotobermuda.com):** The official website of the Bermuda Tourism Authority is a treasure trove of information for travelers. Here, you'll find detailed guides, up-to-date event listings, travel tips, and insights into the island's culture, history, and natural beauty. The website also offers interactive maps, hotel and restaurant recommendations, and practical information to help you plan and navigate your Bermuda adventure.

b) **Bermuda** **Department** **of** **Tourism** **(www.bermudatourism.com):** The Bermuda Department of Tourism's website is another valuable resource for travelers seeking in-depth information about the island. From practical travel advice to an overview of attractions and activities, this website covers a wide range of topics to assist you in creating an unforgettable Bermuda experience. It also provides information on upcoming festivals, local events, and cultural happenings.

2. Guidebooks:

a) **"Bermuda Travel Guide" by Lonely Planet:** Lonely Planet's comprehensive guidebook offers an in-depth exploration of Bermuda, providing detailed insights into the island's history, culture, and attractions. It includes practical advice on accommodations, dining options, transportation, and suggested itineraries for different interests and durations. The guidebook is a valuable companion for those who want a comprehensive and reliable resource at their fingertips.

b) "Insight Guides: Bermuda" by Insight Guides:
This visually stunning guidebook captures the essence of
Bermuda, offering inspiring photographs and expertly
written content. It delves into the island's unique
characteristics, from its natural wonders and vibrant
culture to its captivating history. With detailed maps,
suggested itineraries, and insider tips, this guidebook is an
excellent resource for those seeking a blend of information
and visual inspiration.

3. Mobile Apps:

a) GoToBermuda App: The official GoToBermuda app
is a handy tool for travelers on the go. It provides access to
a wealth of information, including interactive maps, event
listings, local deals, and recommendations for dining,
shopping, and activities. This application enables you to
design a personalized schedule, explore nearby tourist

destinations, and stay informed about the latest events and promotions. It's available for both iOS and Android devices, ensuring that you have valuable information at your fingertips throughout your Bermuda adventure.

b) Bermuda Travel and Explore App: This comprehensive mobile app offers a wealth of information to enhance your Bermuda experience. It provides detailed guides to attractions, beaches, nature reserves, historical landmarks, and practical information on transportation, accommodations, and dining options. The app also includes offline maps, ensuring you can navigate the island without an internet connection. It's available for iOS and Android devices, making it a valuable tool for exploring Bermuda at your own pace.

These additional resources complement the information in "Travel Guide Bermuda: Discover the Secrets of the Atlantic Jewel." They offer a wealth of information, insights, and tools to assist you in planning and navigating your Bermuda adventure. From official tourism websites to trusted guidebooks and convenient mobile apps, these resources ensure you have the knowledge and support to make the most of your time on the island.

As you explore these resources, use them as a starting point for your discoveries. Embrace the island's secrets, immerse yourself in its beauty, and let the additional resources be your companions in unlocking the hidden wonders of the Atlantic Jewel.

So, armed with these valuable resources, embark on your ultimate journey through Bermuda. Dive into the websites, guidebooks, and mobile apps, and let them inspire you to delve deeper into the island's treasures. If you're in search of useful information, expert advice, or visual inspiration, these resources will be your trusted companion as you explore the hidden gems of Bermuda and make unforgettable memories that you'll cherish forever.

CHAPTER 15: CONCLUSION

As we conclude "Travel Guide Bermuda: Discover the Secrets of the Atlantic Jewel," we hope this journey has ignited your passion for exploration, provided valuable insights, and inspired you to embark on your ultimate journey through Bermuda. It has been our pleasure to guide you through this Atlantic paradise's hidden treasures, captivating landscapes, and vibrant culture.

Bermuda, with its pink sand beaches, turquoise waters, and warm hospitality, holds a special place in the hearts of travelers. As soon as you step onto the island, you become a part of its fabric, woven with a deep history, varied traditions, and breathtaking natural scenery that will leave an unforgettable impression on your spirit.

Throughout this guide, we have uncovered the secrets of Bermuda, sharing with you its breathtaking attractions, exhilarating activities, and delectable cuisine. We have provided you with essential information on accommodations, transportation, safety, and local customs, equipping you with the knowledge to navigate the island confidently and easily. From the historic streets of St. George's to the bustling city of Hamilton, from the tranquil nature reserves to the vibrant cultural events, we have unveiled the tapestry that makes Bermuda a truly unique destination.

But our journey does not end here. Bermuda is a place that begs to be explored, experienced, and cherished. As you venture forth, we encourage you to embrace the spirit of discovery and immerse yourself in all that this extraordinary island has to offer. Engage with the locals, savor the flavors of the local cuisine, and let the rhythms of the island's culture move you.

While this guide has provided a comprehensive roadmap, we encourage you to deviate from it and follow your path. Serendipity often leads to the most unforgettable moments, and Bermuda is a place where surprises and hidden gems await around every corner. Take the time to wander, get lost in the narrow streets, and seek out the lesser-known attractions. In these moments of spontaneity, Bermuda's true essence reveals itself.

As you bid farewell to Bermuda, take a moment to reflect on the memories you have created and the connections you have made. The Atlantic Jewel has left its mark on you, and you have left your mark on it. Take the essence of Bermuda along with you on your journey, and let it be a constant reminder of the stunning splendor that exists in our world and the boundless opportunities that await those who pursue them.

We would like to express our sincere gratitude for joining us on this journey, on behalf of the author Brian K. Kirby and the team behind "Travel Guide Bermuda: Discover the Secrets of the Atlantic Jewel." We hope this guide has enriched your experience, provided valuable insights, and sparked a lifelong love affair with Bermuda.

Remember, the secrets of Bermuda are meant to be shared. Share your stories, your experiences, and your newfound knowledge with others. Inspire them to embark on their adventure through the Atlantic Jewel and let the tapestry of Bermuda continue to weave its magic in the hearts of travelers for generations to come.

As you venture into new horizons, we wish you safe travels, thrilling adventures, and unforgettable moments. May the memories of your ultimate journey through Bermuda remain etched in your heart, constantly reminding you of the beauty, wonder, and magic that await those who dare to explore.

Farewell, dear traveler, and may your next voyage be filled with the same awe and wonder that Bermuda has bestowed upon you.

Printed in Great Britain
by Amazon

26196617R00056